CHILDREN'S TRUE STORIES

Surviving Tornadoes

Elizabeth Raum

www.raintreepublishers.co.uk
Visit our website to find out more information about Raintree books.

To order:
☎ Phone 0845 6044371
🖷 Fax +44 (0) 1865 312263
🖳 Email myorders@raintreepublishers.co.uk

Customers from outside the UK please telephone +44 1865 312262

Raintree is an imprint of **Capstone Global Library Limited**, a company incorporated in England and Wales having its registered office at 7 Pilgrim Street, London, EC4V 6LB – Registered company number: 6695582

Text © Capstone Global Library Limited 2011
First published in hardback in 2011
The moral rights of the proprietor have been asserted.

Edited by Louise Galpine and Laura Knowles
Designed by Victoria Allen
Original illustrations © Capstone Global Library
    Limited 2011
Illustrated by HLSTUDIOS
Picture research by Ruth Blair
Originated by Capstone Global Library Limited
Printed and bound in China by CTPS

ISBN 978 1 406 22215 9 (hardback)
15 14 13 12 11
10 9 8 7 6 5 4 3 2 1

British Library Cataloguing in Publication Data

Raum, Elizabeth.
Surviving tornadoes. -- (Children's true stories. Natural disasters)
363.3'4923-dc22
A full catalogue record for this book is available from the British Library.

Acknowledgements
We would like to thank the following for permission to reproduce photographs: Alamy p. 17 (© Trinity Mirror/Mirrorpix), Corbis pp. 5 (© Jim Reed), 12 (© Bettmann), 13 (© Bettmann), 18 (© Andrew Fox), 22 (© Larry W. Smith/epa), 23 (© Larry W. Smith/epa); © Doug Dokken p. 7; Getty Images pp. 15 (Michael Mauney Time Life Pictures), 21 (Jim Reed/Science Faction), 24 (Joshua Lott/Bloomberg), 25 (AFP); NOAA pp. 4 (National Severe Storms Laboratory (NSSL)), 8, 11; PA Photos pp. 19 (© Rui Vieira/PA Archive), 26 (© Paula Merritt/AP).

Cover photograph of a storm chaser planting a weather probe in the path of a tornado near Woonsocket, South Dakota, USA, reproduced with permission of Getty Images/Peter Carsten/National Geographic.

Natasha West's story on page 17 is from Rhona Ganguly, "Tornado Strikes: In Case I'm Killed, Mum – I love You; Evacuees Relive the Nightmare," *Birmingham Evening Mail*, July 30, 2005. Quotations on page 18 and 19 are from Andy Shipley, "Tornado Strikes: Spirit of the Blitz; Families Pull Together for Clean-up," *Birmingham Evening Mail*, July 30, 2005.

The author would like to thank Doug Dokken, Stever Berger, Cecelia (Lehman) Emery, Mariah Charlton and her mother for so generously sharing their stories.

We would like to thank Daniel Block for his invaluable help in the preparation of this book.

Every effort has been made to contact copyright holders of material reproduced in this book. Any omissions will be rectified in subsequent printings if notice is given to the publisher.

Disclaimer

Contents

DAILY LIFE

Read here to learn about what life was like for the children in these stories, and the impact the disaster had at home and school.

NUMBER CRUNCHING

Find out here the details about natural disasters and the damage they cause.

Survivors' lives

Read these boxes to find out what happened to the children in this book when they grew up.

HELPING HAND

Find out how people and organizations have helped to save lives.

On the scene

Read eyewitness accounts of the natural disasters in the survivors' own words.

Some words are printed in bold, **like this**. You can find out what they mean by looking in the glossary on page 30.

Introduction

Tornadoes are the most violent storms on Earth. They can destroy homes, toss lorries into the air, and flatten entire towns. Children who have lived through tornadoes never forget the experience. Some find ways to protect themselves from future storms. Others spend their lives studying tornadoes.

This tornado touched down in Texas, USA in 1995. It is in contact with both the ground and the cloud above.

NUMBER-CRUNCHING

About 1,300 tornadoes strike the United States each year. That's about three quarters of all the tornadoes worldwide. Even so, only about 1 in 100 Americans will ever see a tornado in person.

What is a tornado?

A tornado is a column of air that **rotates** (twists) at a great speed. Tornadoes are sometimes called "twisters". Tornadoes often begin as **supercell thunderstorms**. Supercell thunderstorms develop when warm, moist air rises to meet colder, dry air which is moving in a different direction. If the rising air, or updraft, begins to rotate, a tornado may occur.

Scientists called **meteorologists** use **radar** to track thunderstorm activity. They try to work out when a tornado will happen so that they can warn people before the tornado strikes.

Supercell thunderstorms, such as this one, often go on to form tornadoes.

Fargo, North Dakota, USA: 1957

On 20 June 1957, seven-year-old Doug Dokken was playing in his back garden with his six-year-old brother, Dickie. The boys' mother called them to come and see a huge cloud in the sky.

The cloud fascinated Doug. It was about 16 kilometres (10 miles) wide and seemed to be turning slowly. Bluish-white lightning flickered continuously inside the cloud. Thunder boomed, and there was a rumbling noise, like an aeroplane.

This map shows which parts of the United States have the most tornadoes each year.

Birthday cake

People came out of their houses with cameras and began taking pictures. Doug described the cloud as "a giant upside-down birthday cake with greenish black frosting melting upward on its side".

Doug Dokken, right, and his brother Dickie, left, witnessed the Fargo tornado.

HELPING HAND

Ray Jensen was the meteorologist on duty in Fargo on 20 June 1957. There were no weather satellites in 1957. Ray Jensen relied on his own eyes. In the sky, he saw a tornado **funnel** drop from a cloud and spin down to the ground. He telephoned the local radio and television stations and read out a warning over the air.

Monstrous creature

Doug's mother saw a tornado drop out of the base of the cloud. She rushed the boys to the basement where they listened to tornado warnings on the radio. Doug later wrote, "I didn't feel threatened by the storm. It was like a monstrous and strange creature from another planet."

Doug's family was lucky – the tornado missed their house. Many others lost their homes or were injured. The Fargo tornado killed thirteen people. Seven of them were children.

These people are trying to save whatever they can after the tornado destroyed their house.

Doug's life now

Doug Dokken is now a maths professor living in Minnesota, USA. He studies supercell thunderstorms, and his work helps scientists understand how tornadoes begin. Doug also enjoys chasing tornadoes. "Storm chasing is like going after a big dangerous animal," he says. "You have to understand what you are looking for and where to go to observe tornadoes safely."

NUMBER-CRUNCHING

In 1971, Dr Ted Fujita developed a system for rating tornadoes based on his study of the Fargo tornado. It was called the Fujita scale. In the United Kingdom, a similar scale is used, called the Torro scale (see chart below). The scale estimates a tornado's wind speed in kilometres or miles per hour, based on the amount of damage caused.

Torro Scale	Wind speed	Damage
T0	61–86 kmph (39–54 mph)	Damage to tents, twigs, roof tiles, garden furniture.
T1	87–115 kmph (55–72 mph)	Damage to sheds, trees, chimneys, windows, small plants.
T2	116–147 kmph (73–92 mph)	Light trailers blown over; sheds destroyed; damage to roofs.
T3	148–184 kmph (93–114 mph)	Mobile homes overturned; garages destroyed; buildings shake.
T4	185–220 kmph (115–136 mph)	Cars lifted; mobile homes destroyed; roofs blown away; trees snapped; signs folded or twisted.
T5	221–259 kmph (137–160 mph)	Heavy cars lifted; bricks torn from houses; weak buildings collapse; utility poles snapped.
T6	260–299 kmph (161–186 mph)	Strong houses damaged or demolished; major debris; objects become missiles.
T7	300–342 kmph (187–212 mph)	Brick and wooden houses destroyed; trains overturned.
T8	343–385 kmph (213–240 mph)	Cars blown great distances; steel buildings damaged or destroyed; heavy debris covers ground.
T9	386–432 kmph (241–269 mph)	Steel buildings destroyed; trains thrown great distances.
T10	433–482 kmph (270–299 mph)	Houses lifted from foundations; major destruction in path.

Super Outbreak, USA: 1974

On the morning of 3 April 1974, meteorologists **predicted** rain and thunderstorms throughout the Eastern and Midwestern United States. However, no one imagined the damage that was about to occur. Over the course of that day and the next, 148 tornadoes touched down in 13 states and a Canadian province, killing 343 people and injuring more than 6,000. In less than 18 hours, 2,331 square kilometres (900 square miles) of property suffered tornado damage. The most deadly tornado struck Xenia, Ohio (see map, below).

This map shows where the Super Outbreak tornadoes touched down. Tennessee, Kentucky, and Indiana experienced the most tornadoes.

Key
- 30–39 tornadoes
- 20–29 tornadoes
- 10–19 tornadoes
- 1–9 tornadoes

0   300 miles
0   300 kilometres

This is a photograph of the tornado that struck the town of Xenia, Ohio.

On the scene

Steve Berger, who lived in Ohio, USA was 10 years old when the Super Outbreak occurred. He never forgot it. "April 3rd was the scariest day of my life," he later wrote. "We all went into the basement and only had a small radio for news. I've never heard so much commotion and fear come out of a little black box. Tornado warnings were constant, and I heard the one for Xenia, too. At the time I felt I was going to die that day."

Cecilia's story

Cecilia Lehman, aged 15, was cooking dinner on 3 April 1974. Her mother rushed home from work. She had heard tornado warnings on the radio. Cecilia's 13-year-old brother ran inside, yelling "the tornado is here!"

Cecilia looked out the window and saw a massive black cloud with blue edges. As she watched, three separate funnels dipped up and down and then joined together to form one huge twister.

Because they had no basement, the family huddled in the hall, away from windows. Cecilia didn't think anything bad would happen. She was wrong.

These people are searching for victims buried beneath the ruins of a neighbourhood in Kentucky.

Lifted

When the tornado hit the house, Cecilia was lying on her stomach on the floor. She felt herself being lifted off the floor as the tornado sucked the carpet out from beneath her. She remembers praying that her family would survive.

This house, just north of Xenia, lost one entire wall in the tornado.

NUMBER-CRUNCHING

Only two per cent of tornadoes are as strong as the tornado that hit Xenia. Most tornadoes last less than 10 minutes. They are most likely to occur between 3.00 p.m. and 9.00 p.m.

Rescue

When the tornado moved on, Cecilia heard her brother calling her name. The family had survived! Denise, aged 10, escaped from the wreckage to get help. Neighbours found Cecilia pinned between a water heater and part of the roof. They took Cecilia and her mum to the hospital.

NUMBER-CRUNCHING

This chart shows the details of the 1974 Super Outbreak:

State or province	Number of tornado touchdowns	Number of deaths	Number of people taken to hospital
Tennessee	38	50	635
Kentucky	25	77	1,377
Indiana	18	49	768
Illinois	13	2	30
Ohio	10	41	2,138
Georgia	9	17	104
Alabama	8	86	949
North Carolina	7	7	74
West Virginia	6	1	32
Michigan	5	3	20
Virginia	5	2	13
Mississippi	2	0	1
New York	1	0	0
Ontario, Canada	1	8	23
Totals	148	343	6,165

Recovery

Despite widespread damage, the people of Xenia were determined to rebuild their town. Bumper stickers proclaimed: "Xenia Lives". Even though seven of the town's twelve school buildings were destroyed, children went back to school after only a few weeks. Eventually, they rebuilt and repaired all the schools. Today, Xenia schools have weather alert radios. They also practise taking shelter so that pupils will know what to do if another tornado strikes Xenia.

Many families lost everything in the tornado, even family photographs.

Cecilia's life now

Today Cecilia works at McKinley Elementary School in Xenia as an **occupational therapist**. She helps children who have physical or learning problems to succeed in school. Living through the tornado made her want to help others who face difficult situations.

Birmingham, UK: 2005

Tornadoes can strike anywhere. While they are most common in the United States, Europe experiences tornadoes, too. People in the United Kingdom report an average of 33 tornadoes a year. Most are weak tornadoes, but even weak tornadoes can cause great damage if they strike areas where people live. The tornado that struck Birmingham, UK, on 28 July 2005 was a T4 tornado with fierce winds (see chart on page 9).

In 2005, a tornado struck Birmingham, UK.

28 July 2005 was a grey and rainy day in Birmingham, but nobody was expecting a tornado.

Natasha's story

Natasha West, aged 14, and her cousin Tammy had just arrived home from shopping when the sky darkened. Natasha's mother rushed the girls inside. The winds were so strong that all three had to push on the door to close it.

As the winds began to rip the house apart, Natasha expected to die. She turned to her mother and told her she loved her. They clung together as broken glass and pieces of the floor flew at them.

The house was totally destroyed, but Natasha, her cousin, and her mum were alive and thankful that they had survived.

The Birmingham tornado sent cars flying. This one was smashed into the side of a house!

Lethanial's story

Lethanial Adam, aged 9, was in a car on his way to a shop when the tornado struck Birmingham. Swirling **debris** – milk crates, boxes, tiles from roofs – clogged the road. Lethanial didn't know what was happening or what to do. "I thought I was going to die," Lethanial said. "I thought that the car was going to be picked up by the wind. I was so scared."

Damage report

Luckily, Lethanial wasn't injured. The car was damaged, and so were many others. Trees and debris blocked the streets. Signs were twisted. Many houses were damaged, too. About 200 people, including 150 children, had to find places to stay until their houses were repaired. Some schools also suffered damage.

The tornado damaged many roofs, making the houses unsafe to live in until they were repaired.

On the scene

Naveed Ahmed, aged 12, was raking up debris when he spoke to a reporter. "The winds just picked up vans and cars and sent them crashing down the street," he said. "It was scary, but now we're helping to get things back to normal."

Greensburg, Kansas, USA: 2007

It was a beautiful sunny day in Greensburg, Kansas on 4 May 2007. Mariah Charlton, aged 11, wasn't worried about the weather when she got home from school.

Everything changed that evening. At 8.55 p.m. the National Weather Service issued a tornado warning for Greensburg. The television weatherman told listeners to go to a safe place, but to first turn up the television so they could continue to hear the warnings.

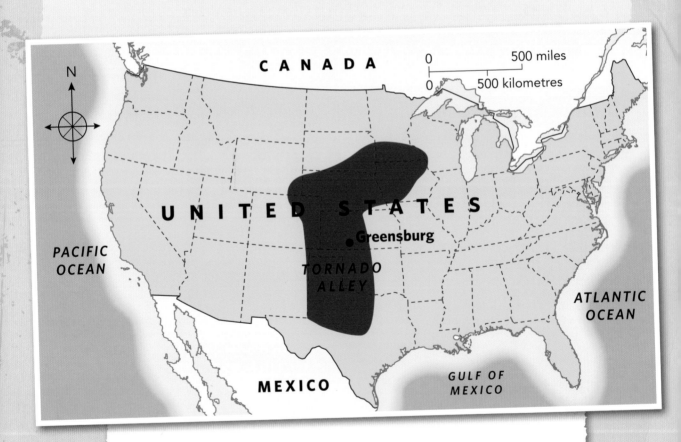

Greensburg is located in "Tornado Alley", an area of the United States where tornadoes are most likely to occur.

Finding shelter

Giant **hailstones** hit the house. Mariah dashed outside, grabbed one, and put it in the freezer. The Charltons had no basement, so Mariah and her parents rushed to the bathroom. A small room, such as a bathroom, in the centre of the house, provides some protection from storms. They covered their heads with pillows and blankets. At 9.45 p.m. the house began to shake.

Large hailstones such as these often fall just before a tornado strikes.

HELPING HAND

The National Weather Service, television and radio weather forecasters, and storm spotters saved lives by issuing weather warnings. People in Greensburg had 26 minutes to seek shelter. Although 95 per cent of Greensburg was destroyed, only 11 of the town's 1,500 people died.

Cracking and popping

Mariah's house cracked and popped as it came apart.
Mariah felt herself being lifted up, and then she was
outside on the ground. It was pitch black.

"I was freezing," Mariah said. Her shirt had ridden up
her back, and when she tried to pull the shirt down, she
couldn't. Something – wood, she thought – was stuck in
her back. Her eyes stung, her mouth was ripped open,
and she had lots of cuts and bruises.

This house, like Mariah's, was completely destroyed by
the tornado that hit Greensburg.

Mum?

Mariah reached out and found a torch. It worked! She still couldn't see her parents, but she heard her mother yell. Both parents were buried underneath the debris from the house.

Neighbours dug Mariah's parents out, and ambulances arrived. Her parents were seriously injured. Mariah had a fish hook stuck in her back. Even though the hook had been inside a locked **tackle box** inside a closed cupboard, the strong winds had sent it flying.

Mariah recovered. So did her parents. But none of them will ever forget the tornado that destroyed Greensburg and nearly cost them their lives.

Most of Greensburg was destroyed by the tornado.

Damage report

The tornado that struck Greensburg was extremely powerful, with winds of up to 330 kilometres per hour (205 miles per hour). It stayed on the ground for about an hour. As it looped through the town it destroyed 961 buildings and damaged about 500 others.

The tornado that struck Greensburg was so strong that it turned this van upside-down.

DAILY LIFE

Today, Mariah feels safe in Greensburg. When her family rebuilt their house, they included a safe room in the basement. This room is made of cement. It has no windows. Double-locks on the door prevent winds from forcing it open. The school, hospital, and other public buildings include safe areas and tornado warning systems.

Good wind

In 2007, the wind destroyed Greensburg. Today, the wind keeps it going. In 2010 the Greensburg Wind Farm began providing enough clean, **renewable** energy to meet the needs of 4,000 households. Every home and business in Greensburg runs on **wind energy**. The town shares leftover wind energy with neighbouring communities.

Green town

Greensburg is the greenest town in the United States. Builders used **recycled materials**, **environmentally friendly** cleaning products, energy-saving light bulbs, and low-flush toilets. The new toilets save the town around 9.5 million litres (2.5 million gallons) of water each year.

Greensburg's new school, which can be seen being built in this photo, uses renewable energy and environmentally friendly building materials.

Conclusion

In the United States, most tornadoes occur during April, May, or June on hot, humid, or stormy days. But tornadoes can occur at any time or anywhere, and often with little or no warning.

Meteorologists and people who study storms, such as Doug Dokken, suggest that everyone should be alert to the weather. Thunderstorms may be a sign that trouble is coming if they have greenish or greenish-black colours, large hailstones, a continuous rumbling that doesn't fade away, or giant, low lying clouds.

Tornadoes do strange things, such as tear down the walls of the house but leave the dishes untouched. That happened to this house in Mississippi, USA in April 2010.

Keeping safe

Some people are fascinated by storms and go outside to take pictures. While storms are exciting, they can also be dangerous. All tornadoes produce a funnel that reaches from the cloud to the ground. If you see a funnel, take shelter immediately, even if the funnel seems far away.

Doug, Cecilia, Natasha, Lethanial, and Mariah are survivors. Their stories teach us what to expect and what to do when a tornado strikes.

HELPING HAND

These are instructions of what to do if you hear a tornado warning or see a tornado funnel. It is important that everyone knows what to do in an emergency – even people who do not live in an area that has many tornadoes.

If you are in a house with a basement	If you are in a house without a basement	If you are in a mobile home	If you are outside or in a car
Go to the basement immediately. Cover yourself with a mattress or blankets. Stay away from windows.	Move to a small room or hallway on the lowest floor and get under a sturdy piece of furniture. Cover yourself with a mattress or blankets. Stay away from windows.	Leave immediately. Go to a nearby shelter if possible. If not, lie on the ground as far from buildings and trees as possible. Cover your head with your arms.	Leave your car immediately. Lie flat in a nearby ditch or dip in the ground. Get as far away from buildings and trees as possible. Cover your head with your arms.

Mapping tornadoes

This map shows where in the world tornadoes are most likely to happen. Although many tornadoes happen in Europe, they are normally very weak.

Fargo, North Dakota, USA

The tornado that hit Fargo in 1957 led to the development of the Fujita Scale to rate tornadoes in the United States. The Fargo tornado was as an F5, the most violent type.

Greensburg, Kansas, USA

The tornado that struck Greensburg in 2007 destroyed the town and left 11 people dead and over 60 injured. Like the Fargo and Xenia tornadoes, it was an F5.

East and Midwest USA

In 1974, 148 tornadoes struck the United States during an 18-hour period. This is called a Super Outbreak. It was the most tornadoes ever reported during any single storm.

Fargo

NORTH AMERICA

Xenia

Greensburg

ATLANTIC OCEAN

PACIFIC OCEAN

SOUTH AMERICA

Birmingham, United Kingdom

Tornadoes can hit anywhere. The tornado which struck Birmingham in 2005 surprised most people as they did not expect a tornado in the United Kingdom.

Birmingham

EUROPE

ASIA

AFRICA

PACIFIC OCEAN

INDIAN OCEAN

AUSTRALASIA

Key

Areas most likely to experience tornadoes

ANTARCTICA

Glossary

debris remains of things that have been broken or destroyed

environmentally friendly not harmful to the environment

funnel cone-shaped rotating cloud

hailstone ball of ice produced by a supercell thunderstorm

meteorologist person who studies the science behind the weather

occupational therapist someone who helps children and adults who have physical, medical, or learning problems to succeed

predict say that something will happen in the future, usually based on research or other information

radar way of seeking out distant objects and working out their position, speed, or other characteristics by turning radio waves into images

recycled material material that is reused for a new purpose, for example, a child's swing made from an old tyre

renewable able to be replaced over time

rotate to spin around a central point

supercell thunderstorm enormous thunderstorm which can create a tornado, rain, and large hail

tackle box box of fishing equipment

wind energy energy produced by the wind, usually through the use of large windmills

Find Out More

Books

Hurricanes and Tornadoes (Natural Disasters), Richard and Louise Spilsbury
(Wayland, 2010)

Terrifying Tornadoes (Awesome Forces of Nature), Louise and Richard Spilsbury
(Raintree, 2010)

Tornadoes and Superstorms (Graphic Natural Disasters), Gary Jeffrey
(Franklin Watts, 2010)

Websites

http://www.weatherwizkids.com/weather-tornado.htm
This website provides tornado information for children, and all kinds
of other weather facts.

kids.nationalgeographic.com/kids/games/geographygames
This National Geographic website has a great quiz about tornadoes.
Look through their list of quizzes and games to find the one about
tornadoes, and many more.

http://eo.ucar.edu/webweather/thunderhome.html
This is a fun site where children can learn about extreme weather,
play games, and do activities.

http://video.kidzui.com/channels/Tornadoes
This website shows children real video footage of tornadoes.

Index